Pebble® Plus

Animals Working Together

Zebras and Oxpeckers Work Together

by Martha E. H. Rustad

Consulting Editor: Gail Saunders-Smith, PhD

Consultant: Jackie Gai, DVM
Zoo and Exotic Animal Consultation

CAPSTONE PRESS
a capstone imprint

Pebble Plus is published by Capstone Press,
151 Good Counsel Drive, P.O. Box 669, Mankato, Minnesota 56002.
www.capstonepub.com

Books published by Capstone Press are manufactured with paper containing at least 10 percent post-consumer waste.

Library of Congress Cataloging-in-Publication Data
Rustad, Martha E. H. (Martha Elizabeth Hillman), 1975–
Zebras and oxpeckers work together / by Martha E. H. Rustad.
   p. cm.—(Pebble plus. Animals working together)
 Includes bibliographical references and index.
 Summary: "Simple text and full-color photographs introduce the symbiotic relationship of zebras and oxpeckers"—Provided by publisher.
 ISBN 978-1-4296-5300-8 (library binding)
 ISBN 978-1-4296-6200-0 (paperback)
 1. Zebras—Ecology—Juvenile literature. 2. Oxpeckers—Ecology—Juvenile literature. 3. Symbiosis—Juvenile literature. I. Title. II. Series.
 QL737.U62R87 2011
 599.665'71785—dc22
                                                          2010025465

Editorial Credits
Erika L. Shores, editor; Bobbie Nuytten, designer; Svetlana Zhurkin, media researcher;
   Laura Manthe, production specialist

Photo Credits
Alamy/Ann and Steve Toon, 10–11; Frank van Egmond, 14–15; Robert Harding Picture Library, 8–9
Corbis/Galen Rowell, 5
Dreamstime/Steffen Foerster, cover, 21
Getty Images/The Image Bank/David Tipling, 7
Photolibrary/Oxford Scientific/Berndt Fischer, 17
Shutterstock/Mogens Trolle, 12–13; Otto Wikus, 1
Visuals Unlimited/Arthur Morris, 19

Note to Parents and Teachers

The Animals Working Together series supports national science standards related to biology. This book describes and illustrates the relationship between zebras and oxpeckers. The images support early readers in understanding the text. The repetition of words and phrases helps early readers learn new words. This book also introduces early readers to subject-specific vocabulary words, which are defined in the Glossary section. Early readers may need assistance to read some words and to use the Table of Contents, Glossary, Read More, Internet Sites, and Index sections of the book.

Printed in the United States of America in North Mankato, Minnesota.
092010
005933CGS11

Table of Contents

Symbiosis. 4

Oxpeckers Help Zebras 10

Zebras Help Oxpeckers 14

Teamwork 20

Glossary 22

Read More 23

Internet Sites. 23

Index 24

Symbiosis

A hungry lion quietly watches

a group of zebras.

The zebras don't see the lion

in the savanna grass.

Will the zebra herd escape?

An oxpecker sees the lion.
It screams and flies off
a zebra's back. The bird lets
the zebras know to run away.
The herd is safe.

Zebras and oxpeckers are animal partners. Each helps the other find food, shelter, or safety. This relationship is called symbiosis.

Oxpeckers Help Zebras

Oxpeckers eat ticks
and lice off zebras.
These parasites suck blood
from zebras and can make
them sick.

Oxpeckers fly up and cry out
if they spy hyenas, cheetahs,
or lions. Zebras hear the cry.
They know to run away
to safety.

Zebras Help Oxpeckers

Oxpeckers find food because of zebras. Oxpeckers eat parasites off zebras. The birds also catch bugs that zebras kick up as they walk.

Oxpeckers sometimes pull
hair off zebras.
They use the soft hair
to line their nests.

Oxpeckers follow zebras to water.

Zebras dig holes in the dry

African savanna to find water.

Oxpeckers also drink

from these watering holes.

Teamwork

Zebras and oxpeckers are
a team. Symbiosis keeps
both animals healthy
and safe.

Glossary

herd—a large group of animals that live together

louse—a tiny insect that lives on people's and animal's skin; lice suck blood from their host; more than one louse is lice

parasite—a small organism that lives on or inside a person or animal

savanna—a flat, grassy area of land with few or no trees

symbiosis—a relationship between two different kinds of animals; the animals live together to help each other find food, shelter, or safety

tick—a tiny animal that sucks blood from other animals by attaching to their skin

Read More

Silverman, Buffy. *You Scratch My Back.* Raintree Fusion. Chicago: Raintree, 2008.

Stone, Lynn M. *Zebras.* Nature Watch. Minneapolis: Lerner Publications, 2009.

Internet Sites

FactHound offers a safe, fun way to find Internet sites related to this book. All of the sites on FactHound have been researched by our staff.

Here's all you do:

Visit *www.facthound.com*

Type in this code: 9781429653008

Check out projects, games and lots more at
www.capstonekids.com

Index

cheetahs, 12

escaping, 4, 6, 12

hair, 16

hyenas, 12

lice, 10

lions, 4, 6, 12

nests, 16

parasites, 10, 14

savannas, 4, 18

symbiosis, 8, 20

ticks, 10

watering holes, 18

Word Count: 186
Grade: 1
Early-Intervention Level: 17